TAKE IT APART
PLANE

By Chris Oxlade

Illustrated by George Fryer

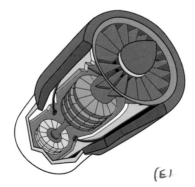

🌸 **Belitha Press**

First Published in the UK in 1996 by
Belitha Press Limited, London House,
Great Eastern Wharf, Parkgate Road,
London SW11 4NQ

ISBN 1 85561 544 4

British Library in Cataloguing in Publication
Data for this book is available from the
British Library.

Printed in China

Editor: Jilly MacLeod
Designer: Guy Callaby
Illustrator: George Fryer
Consultants: Lindsay Peacock and
 Elizabeth Atkinson

Inside this Book

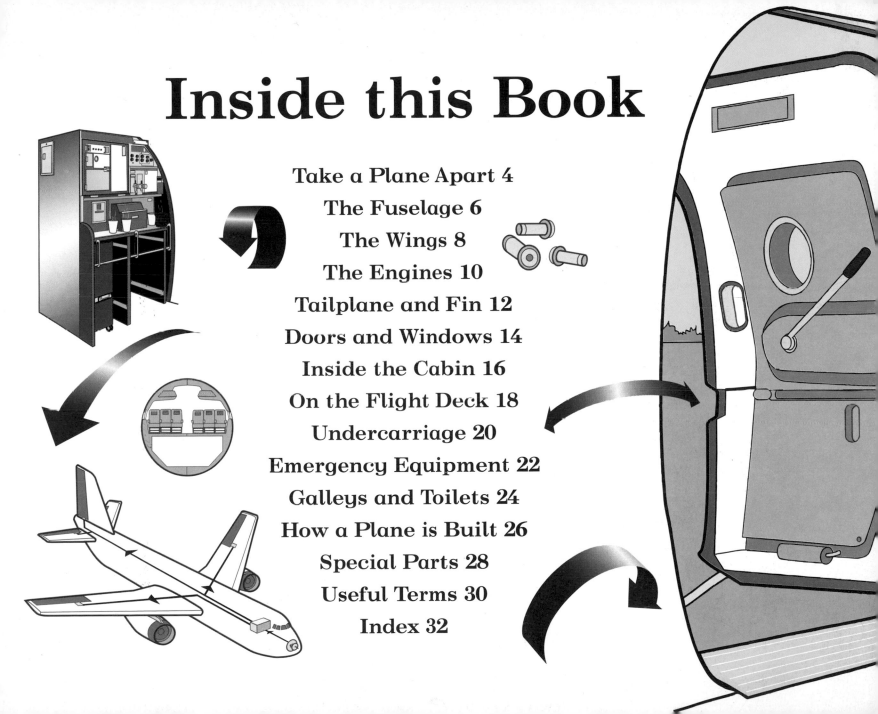

Take a Plane Apart 4

The Fuselage 6

The Wings 8

The Engines 10

Tailplane and Fin 12

Doors and Windows 14

Inside the Cabin 16

On the Flight Deck 18

Undercarriage 20

Emergency Equipment 22

Galleys and Toilets 24

How a Plane is Built 26

Special Parts 28

Useful Terms 30

Index 32

Take a Plane Apart

⊖ A plane is made of tens of thousands of different parts.

⊖ The parts are made of metal, plastic, rubber, glass and many other special materials.

⊖ All the parts are put together in an aircraft factory.

⊘ This book shows you the main parts of an airliner (a large passenger plane) and how they fit together.

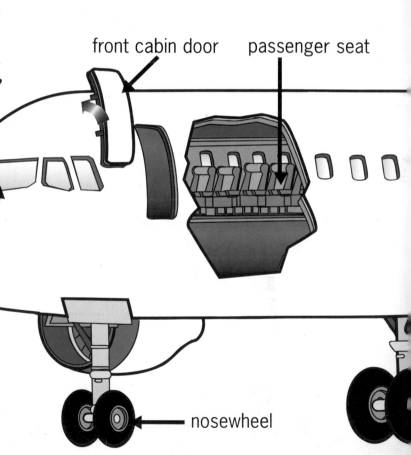

front cabin door

passenger seat

flight deck

nosewheel

4

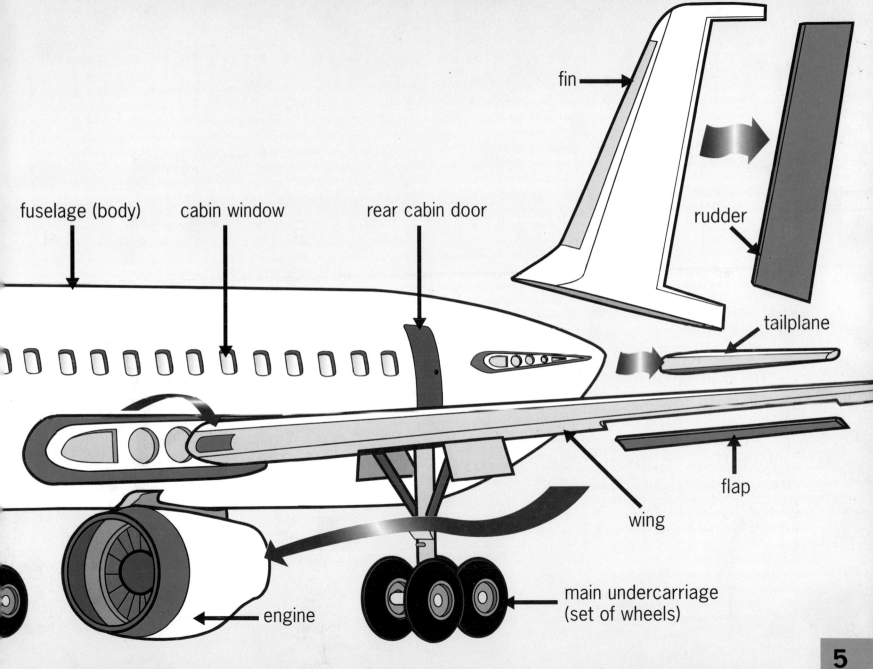

fin

rudder

fuselage (body)

cabin window

rear cabin door

tailplane

wing

flap

engine

main undercarriage
(set of wheels)

The Fuselage

⬤ The fuselage is the main part of the plane where the passengers sit and their baggage is stored.

⬤ The fuselage is a large metal tube. All the other parts of the plane are fixed on to the fuselage.

⬤ The fuselage is filled with air so that the passengers can breathe.

⬤ At the front of the fuselage is the flight deck where the pilot and co-pilot sit.

Fact Box
The Boeing 747 has two passenger decks. Passengers go upstairs to reach the top deck.

Joining the parts
Metal studs called rivets are used to join the metal parts of the plane together.

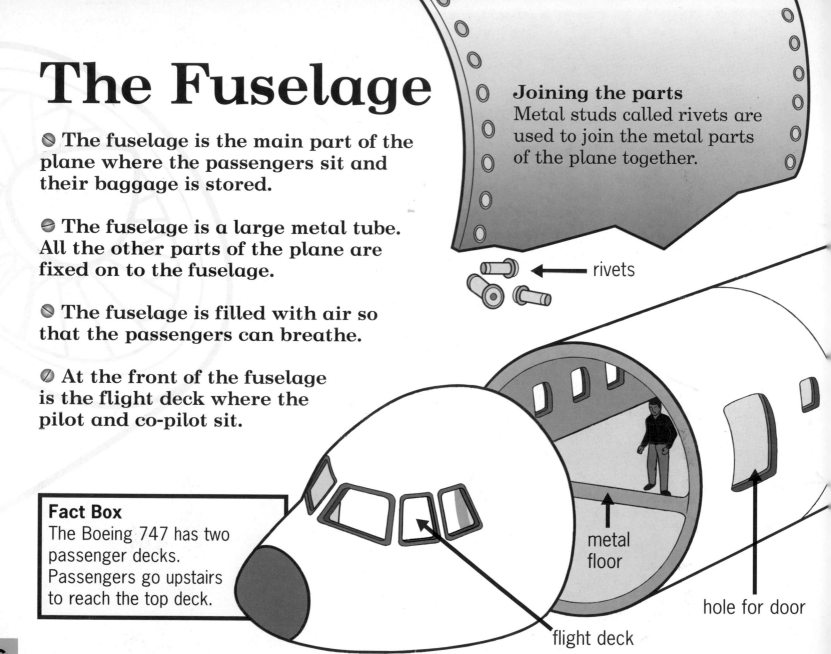

← rivets

metal floor

flight deck

hole for door

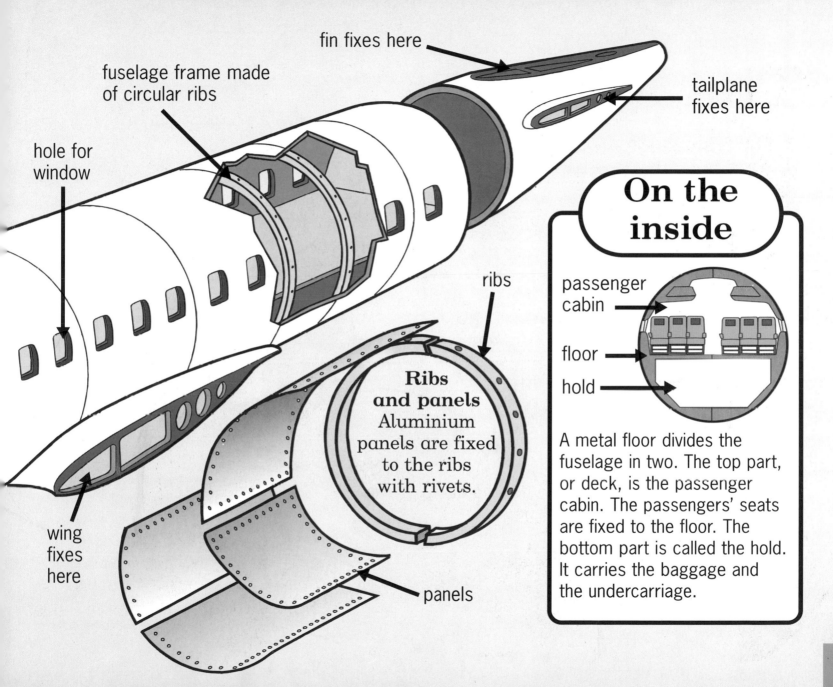

fin fixes here

fuselage frame made of circular ribs

tailplane fixes here

hole for window

On the inside

ribs

passenger cabin

floor

hold

Ribs and panels
Aluminium panels are fixed to the ribs with rivets.

A metal floor divides the fuselage in two. The top part, or deck, is the passenger cabin. The passengers' seats are fixed to the floor. The bottom part is called the hold. It carries the baggage and the undercarriage.

wing fixes here

panels

7

The Wings

● The wings lift the plane into the air and keep it airborne (up in the air).

● The wings are made of metal ribs and spars covered in metal panels.

● On the front and back of the wings are movable pieces that go in and out, or up and down.

● The pilot uses these movable pieces to control the plane.

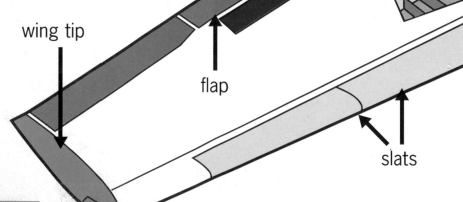

flap

rib

spar

wing tip

flap

slats

Fact Box
Fuel for the engines is stored in the wings, in the spaces between the ribs and spars. The fuel is carried to the engines along fuel pipes.

Moving parts

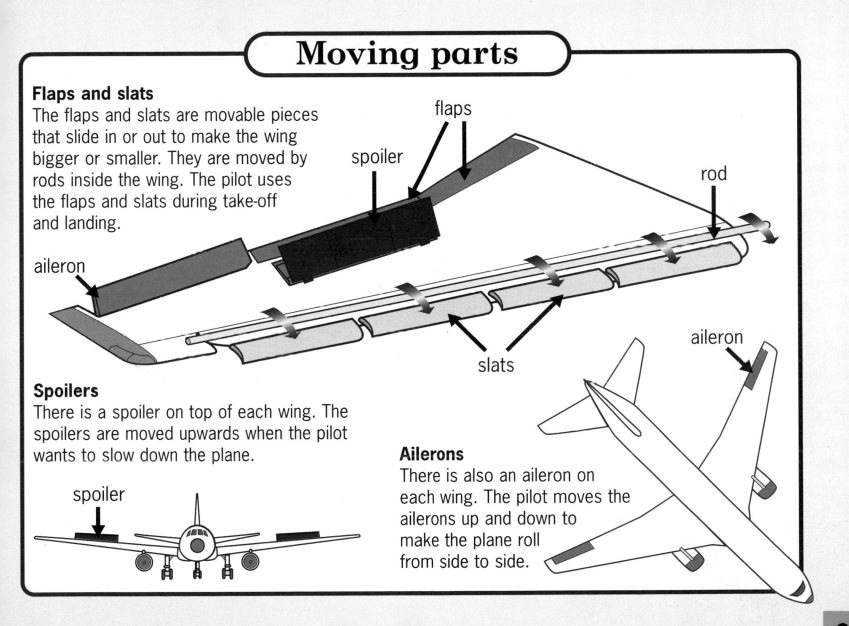

Flaps and slats

The flaps and slats are movable pieces that slide in or out to make the wing bigger or smaller. They are moved by rods inside the wing. The pilot uses the flaps and slats during take-off and landing.

flaps

spoiler

rod

aileron

slats

aileron

Spoilers

There is a spoiler on top of each wing. The spoilers are moved upwards when the pilot wants to slow down the plane.

spoiler

Ailerons

There is also an aileron on each wing. The pilot moves the ailerons up and down to make the plane roll from side to side.

The Engines

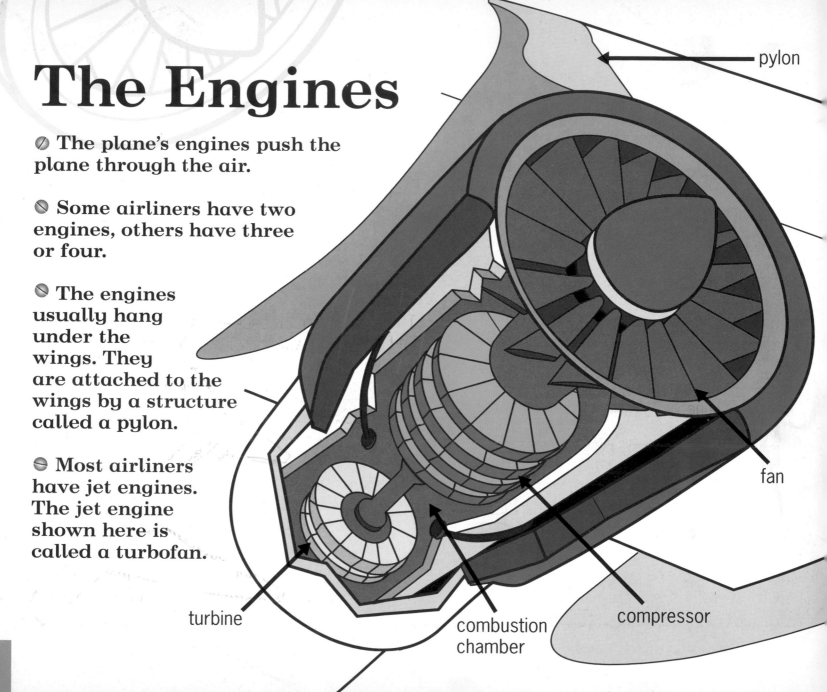

⊘ The plane's engines push the plane through the air.

◉ Some airliners have two engines, others have three or four.

◉ The engines usually hang under the wings. They are attached to the wings by a structure called a pylon.

◉ Most airliners have jet engines. The jet engine shown here is called a turbofan.

pylon

fan

turbine

combustion chamber

compressor

Ground power engine
There is also a small engine inside the tail. It works like the main engines but does not help the plane to fly. Instead, it makes electricity for the plane when it is on the ground.

ground power engine

How a jet engine works

1 Fan
A turbofan jet engine has a huge spinning fan at the front which sucks in air. Most of the air rushes straight through, but some air goes into the engine.

air in

4 Turbine
The hot gases rush backwards out of the engine and drive the plane forwards. The gases also turn the turbine which makes the fan and the compressor spin round.

hot gases out

2 Compressor
A spinning part inside the engine, called a compressor, squeezes the air into the combustion chamber.

3 Combustion chamber
Inside the combustion chamber, the air is used to burn fuel. As the fuel burns, it makes a stream, or jet, of hot gases.

Tailplane and Fin

⊘ The tailplane keeps the plane flying level.

⊘ The fin stops the plane swaying from side to side.

⊘ There is a movable piece on the fin called the rudder, and two on the tailplane called the elevators.

⊘ The pilot uses the rudder and elevators to steer the plane.

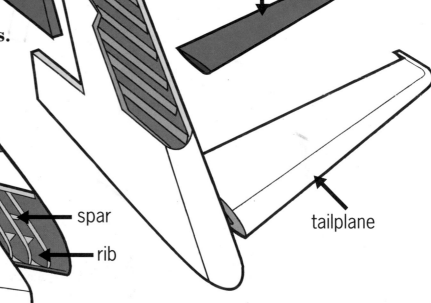

rudder

fin

elevator

tailplane

tailplane

outer skin

spar

rib

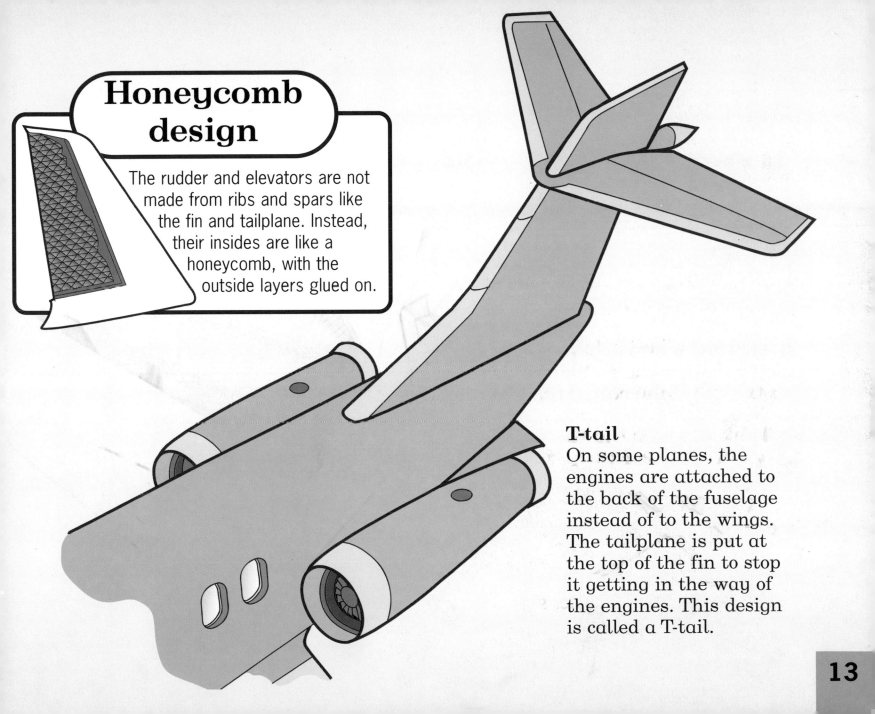

Honeycomb design

The rudder and elevators are not made from ribs and spars like the fin and tailplane. Instead, their insides are like a honeycomb, with the outside layers glued on.

T-tail

On some planes, the engines are attached to the back of the fuselage instead of to the wings. The tailplane is put at the top of the fin to stop it getting in the way of the engines. This design is called a T-tail.

Doors and Windows

● The passengers get on and off the plane through cabin doors in the side of the fuselage.

● The doors are tightly closed before the plane takes off.

● Huge doors under the plane open into the baggage hold.

● There are windows along both sides of the cabin and at the front of the flight deck.

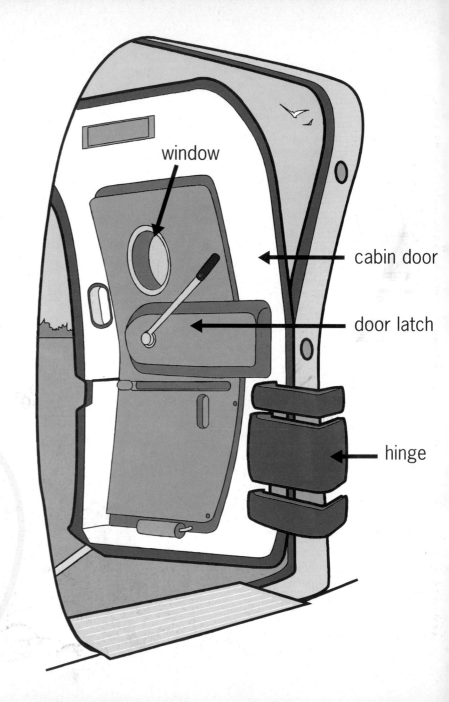

window

cabin door

door latch

hinge

Getting on and off

Small airliners have their own set of stairs – called airstairs – which are pulled down to let passengers on or off the plane. The airstairs fold up and slide under the door when they are not in use.

Passengers usually board airliners through a special tunnel leading from the airport building.

Airstairs

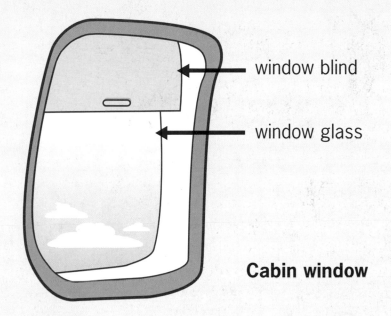

window blind

window glass

Cabin window

Flight deck windows

The windows in the flight deck give the pilot and co-pilot a good all-round view. They are much bigger than the passenger windows, and have very thick glass.

Fact Box

The flight deck windows even have windscreen wipers, just like a car.

Inside the Cabin

◉ The cabin contains rows of seats for the passengers.

◉ Each seat has a seat belt for safety.

◉ In front of each passenger is a fold-down tray and a magazine rack.

◉ Above the passengers' heads are cupboards, called overhead lockers, for coats and bags.

Fact Box
The seats and other parts of the cabin are made of materials that do not burn easily. This helps to prevent fires from starting.

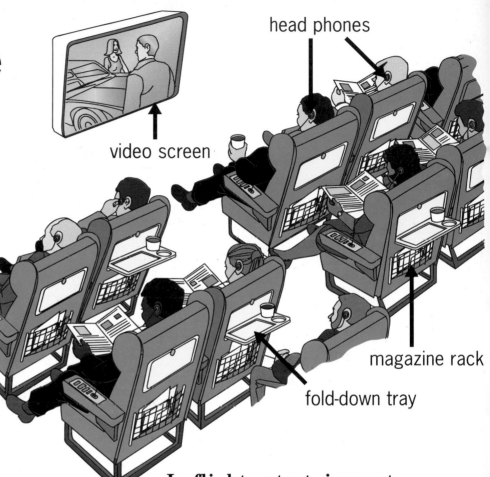

head phones

video screen

magazine rack

fold-down tray

In-flight entertainment
To stop the passengers getting bored on long flights, they are given music to listen to or films to watch on video screens. Passengers listen in to this 'in-flight entertainment' using headphones.

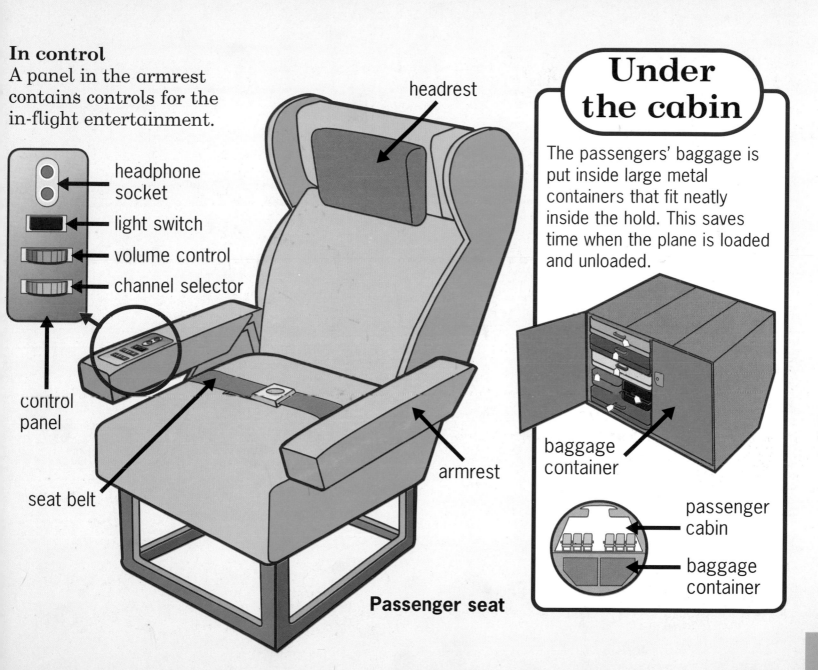

In control
A panel in the armrest contains controls for the in-flight entertainment.

headphone socket

light switch

volume control

channel selector

control panel

seat belt

headrest

armrest

Passenger seat

Under the cabin

The passengers' baggage is put inside large metal containers that fit neatly inside the hold. This saves time when the plane is loaded and unloaded.

baggage container

passenger cabin

baggage container

On the Flight Deck

● **The flight deck is where the pilot and co-pilot sit.**

● **It contains all the controls and switches that the pilots need to fly the plane.**

● **Instruments give the pilots information about the plane, such as how much fuel is left, and how fast it is going.**

● **Many kilometres of electric wiring lead from the flight deck to all parts of the plane.**

Radar screen

Weather detector
At the front of the plane is an electronic machine called a radar. It can detect bad weather ahead. The pilots view the radar pictures on a screen on the flight deck.

Fly-by-wire

In older airliners, pilots control the flaps, slats and other movable parts directly, using a system of rods and levers. In some modern airliners, the movable parts are controlled by computers instead. This is called fly-by-wire.

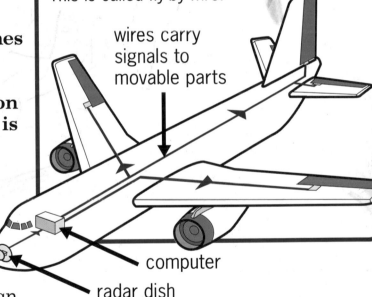

wires carry signals to movable parts

computer

radar dish

18

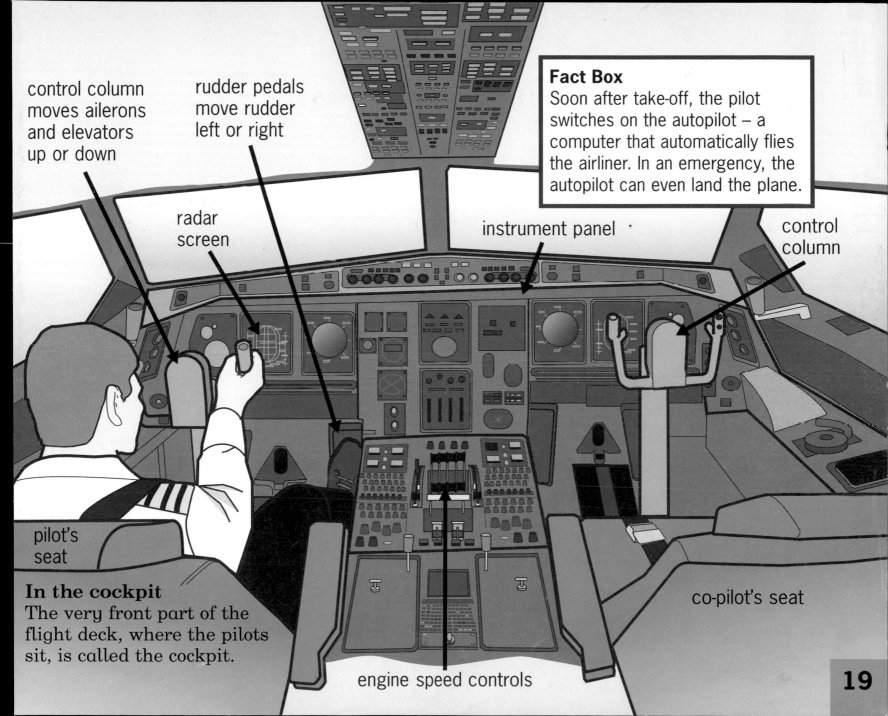

control column moves ailerons and elevators up or down

rudder pedals move rudder left or right

Fact Box
Soon after take-off, the pilot switches on the autopilot – a computer that automatically flies the airliner. In an emergency, the autopilot can even land the plane.

radar screen

instrument panel

control column

pilot's seat

In the cockpit
The very front part of the flight deck, where the pilots sit, is called the cockpit.

co-pilot's seat

engine speed controls

19

Undercarriage

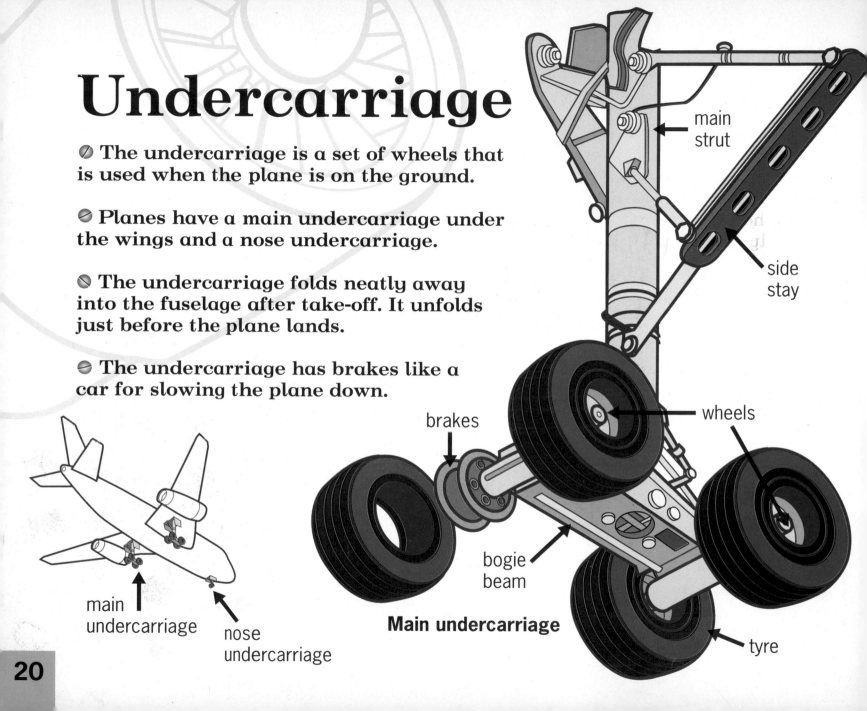

- The undercarriage is a set of wheels that is used when the plane is on the ground.

- Planes have a main undercarriage under the wings and a nose undercarriage.

- The undercarriage folds neatly away into the fuselage after take-off. It unfolds just before the plane lands.

- The undercarriage has brakes like a car for slowing the plane down.

main strut

side stay

brakes

wheels

bogie beam

tyre

main undercarriage

nose undercarriage

Main undercarriage

Undercarriage doors

After take-off, the undercarriage folds away into a hole in the fuselage and wing. Doors close over the hole to give the plane a smooth shape so that it cuts cleanly through the air.

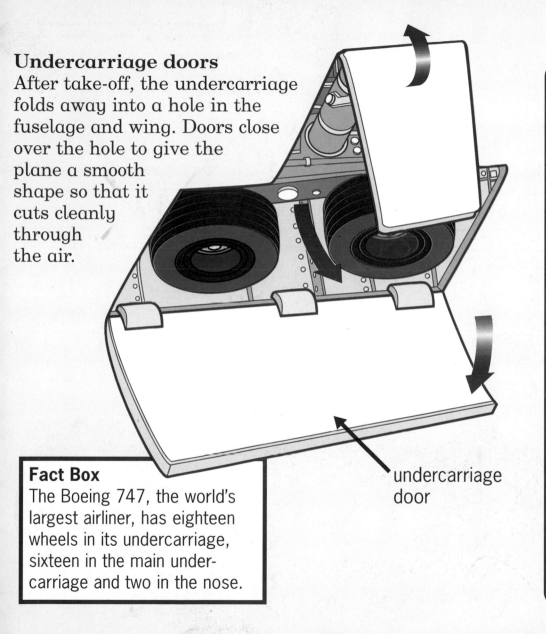

undercarriage door

Fact Box

The Boeing 747, the world's largest airliner, has eighteen wheels in its undercarriage, sixteen in the main under-carriage and two in the nose.

Tyres

An airliner lands at over 200 kilometres an hour. When the tyres hit the runway they get very hot. If they were filled with air the tyres might explode, so they are filled with a special gas instead.

Emergency Equipment

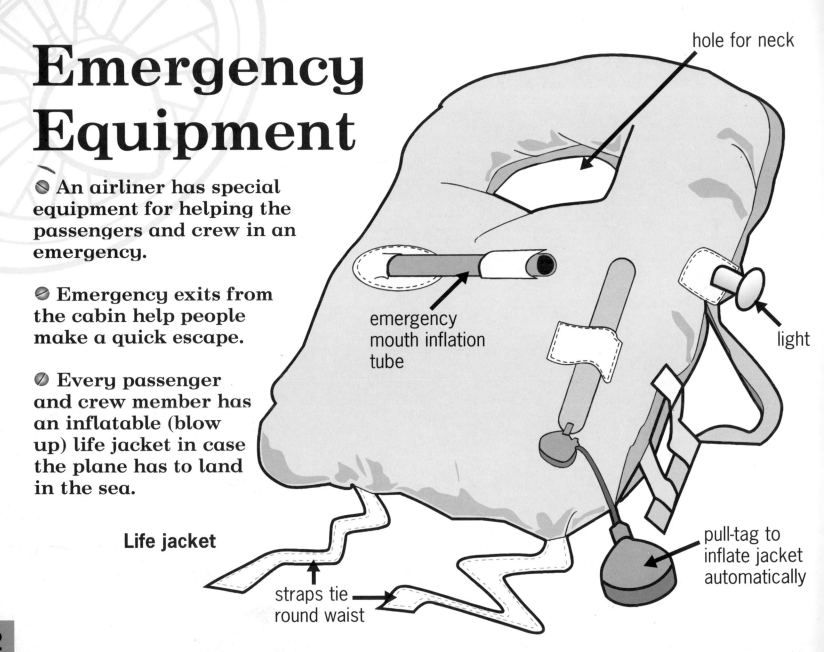

● An airliner has special equipment for helping the passengers and crew in an emergency.

● Emergency exits from the cabin help people make a quick escape.

● Every passenger and crew member has an inflatable (blow up) life jacket in case the plane has to land in the sea.

Life jacket

hole for neck

light

emergency mouth inflation tube

pull-tag to inflate jacket automatically

straps tie round waist

Oxygen masks

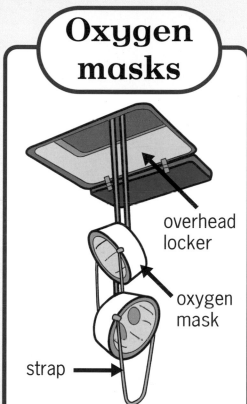

overhead locker

oxygen mask

strap

Oxygen masks are stored in the overhead lockers. They fall down automatically if the air escapes from the cabin. Passengers strap the masks over their nose and mouth to breathe in oxygen.

Emergency slides

If passengers have to leave the cabin quickly, emergency slides are used. The slides are stored in a box inside the cabin doors.

emergency slide

Life rafts

Some planes carry inflatable life rafts, in case the plane has to land in the sea.

Fact Box

Aircraft engines have their own fire extinguishers. If an engine catches fire, the pilot operates the fire extinguishers from the flight deck.

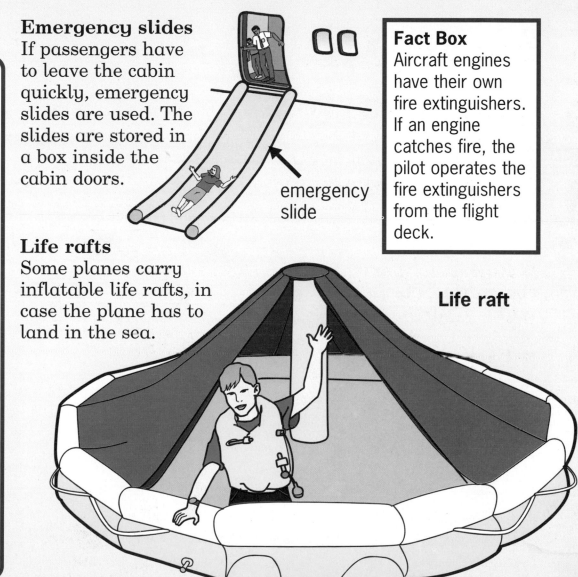

Life raft

Galleys and Toilets

⊘ **The galley is where the cabin staff prepare meals for the passengers.**

⊘ **The galley has microwave ovens, kettles and places to store food and drinks.**

⊘ **Hot meals are cooked before they are put on the plane. They are stored in heated containers in the galley.**

⊘ **The washrooms have toilets and washbasins for the passengers.**

Fact Box
On a Boeing 747 flight from New York to London, the cabin crew may serve over a thousand meals to the passengers.

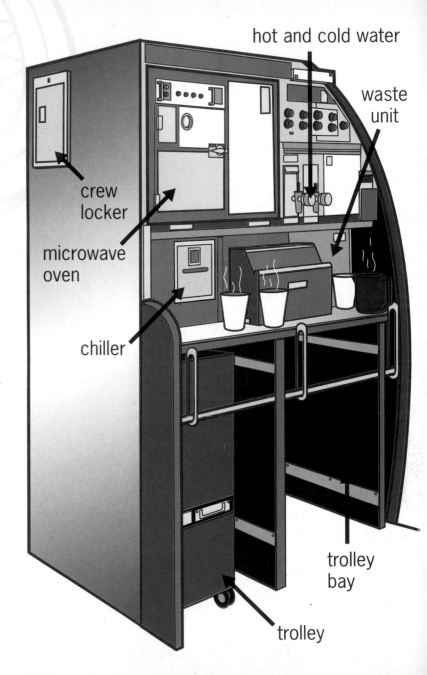

hot and cold water

waste unit

crew locker

microwave oven

chiller

trolley bay

trolley

Feeding the passengers

Food and drinks are taken on trolleys to the passengers. Each person is given a tray complete with food, cutlery, a napkin, cup and glass, and is offered a choice of drinks. When the trolleys are not being used, they are locked into place in the galley.

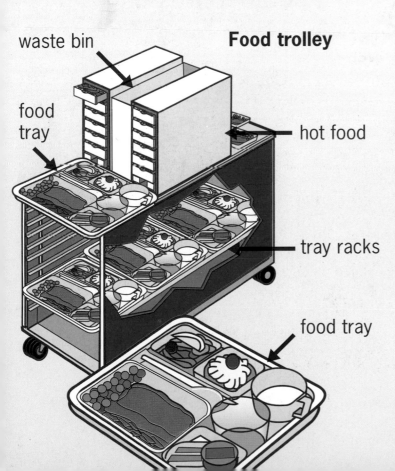

Food trolley

waste bin

food tray

hot food

tray racks

food tray

Huge tanks in the hold store any waste from the toilets until the plane lands at an airport. Then the waste is sucked on to a truck and taken away for disposal.

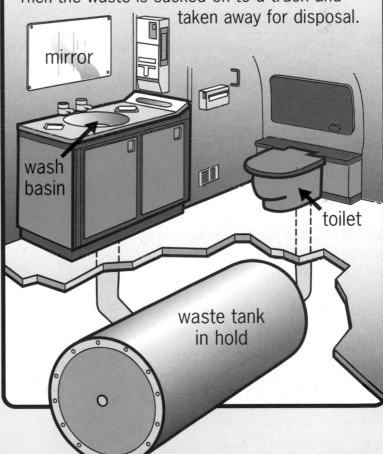

mirror

wash basin

toilet

waste tank in hold

How a Plane is Built

● Airliners are very large and have to be put together in enormous buildings.

● Different parts of the plane are made in different factories. Then they are taken to the main factory to be put together.

● It takes many months to build a plane.

The fuselage and wings
The fuselage is made from short sections joined together. The wings fit to the middle section. All the parts rest on special supports.

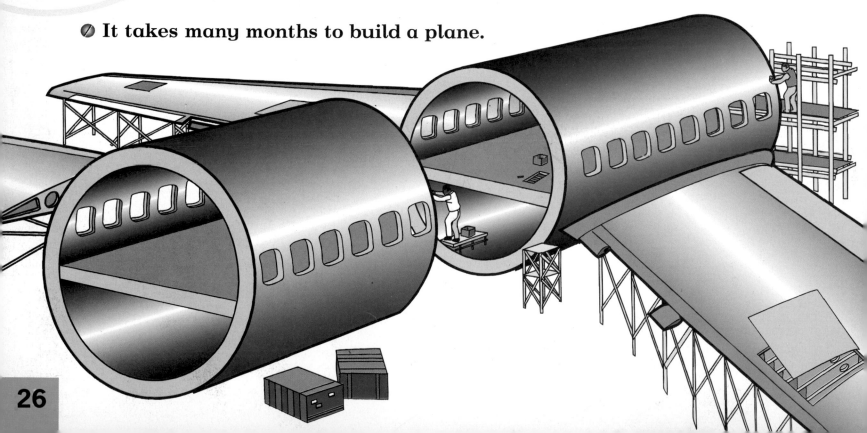

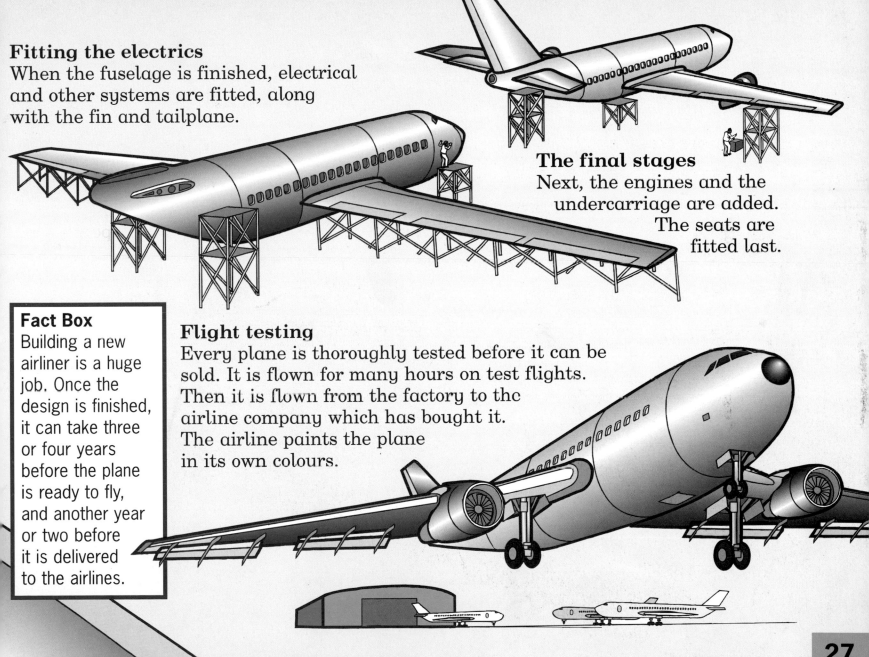

Fitting the electrics

When the fuselage is finished, electrical and other systems are fitted, along with the fin and tailplane.

The final stages

Next, the engines and the undercarriage are added. The seats are fitted last.

Fact Box

Building a new airliner is a huge job. Once the design is finished, it can take three or four years before the plane is ready to fly, and another year or two before it is delivered to the airlines.

Flight testing

Every plane is thoroughly tested before it can be sold. It is flown for many hours on test flights. Then it is flown from the factory to the airline company which has bought it. The airline paints the plane in its own colours.

Special Parts

⚙ Some planes do special jobs.

⚙ They have different parts from other planes or extra parts which most planes do not have.

⚙ You can see some of these special parts on this spread.

Floats
In countries where there are many lakes, such as Canada, planes have to be able to land on water. They have floats on their undercarriage instead of wheels.

Propellers
Many planes have propellers on their engines to drive the plane forwards. Propeller-powered planes are not as fast as jets but they use less fuel and are cheaper to run.

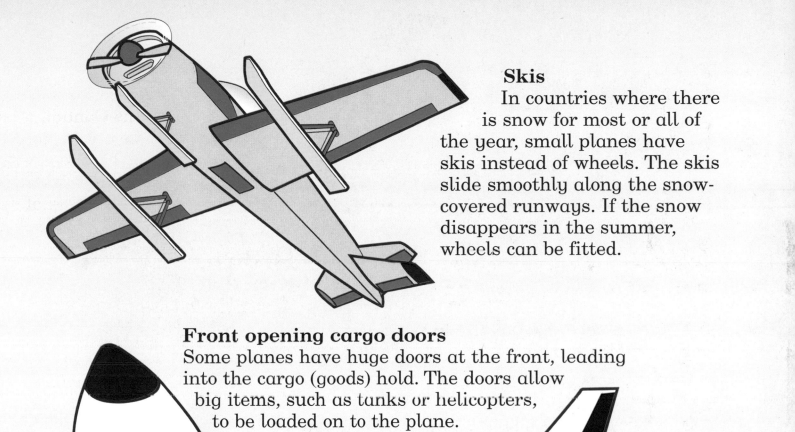

Skis

In countries where there is snow for most or all of the year, small planes have skis instead of wheels. The skis slide smoothly along the snow-covered runways. If the snow disappears in the summer, wheels can be fitted.

Front opening cargo doors

Some planes have huge doors at the front, leading into the cargo (goods) hold. The doors allow big items, such as tanks or helicopters, to be loaded on to the plane.

Useful Terms

aileron A panel towards the end of a plane's wing that is moved up or down to make the plane roll from side to side.

autopilot A computer that flies the plane automatically without the pilot's help.

baggage hold A space in the fuselage where the passengers' cases and bags are stored during a flight. It is normally under the cabin floor.

cockpit The front part of a plane's flight deck. It is where the pilot and co-pilot sit, surrounded by controls and instruments.

control column The control which the pilot holds when he or she is flying a plane. It controls the elevators and ailerons.

elevator A part on the back edge of the tailplane that is moved up and down to make the plane climb or descend.

fin The upright piece at the back of the fuselage. It helps to keep the plane flying straight.

flap A movable part on the back edge of the wing that slides out to make the wing bigger. The flaps are used during take-off and landing.

flight deck The room at the front of a plane where the pilots sit and where all the plane's controls and instruments are.

fuselage The main part of a plane, where passengers sit and cargo is carried. All the other parts are attached to the fuselage.

galley A small kitchen in an airliner's cabin. Cabin staff prepare food and drinks in the galley.

ground power engine A small jet engine that makes electricity for the plane while the main engines are turned off.

jet engine A type of plane engine that sends a stream, or jet, of hot gases backwards at very high speed. This pushes the plane forwards.

life raft An inflatable (blow-up) boat used in case a plane has to make an emergency landing at sea.

propeller engine An engine that makes a propeller (a set of long blades) spin round. This pushes the plane forwards.

pylon The part of a plane that connects the plane's engines to its wings.

radar An electronic machine that is used to detect other planes nearby and bad weather.

rib A hoop of metal in a plane's fuselage. Rows of ribs make up the frame of the fuselage. Metal panels are attached to the ribs to form an outer shell.

rivet A metal fastener used for joining two pieces of metal together.

rudder A part on the back of a fin that is turned from side to side to make the plane turn from side to side.

slat A part on the front edge of the wing that slides out to make the wing bigger during take-off and landing.

spar Part of a wing's frame that stretches from one end of the wing to the other. Spars stop the wing bending too much.

spoiler A part on the back of the wing that lifts up to slow the plane down before it lands.

tailplane The small pair of wings at the back of the fuselage. The tailplane helps the plane to fly level.

turbofan A type of jet engine that is often used on large planes. It has a large fan in front of the engine to suck in air.

undercarriage Sets of wheels under the plane that the plane rolls along on while it is on the ground. On large planes, the undercarriage folds away when the plane is flying. Smaller planes have a fixed undercarriage which does not fold away.

Index

aileron 9, 19, 30
aircraft factory 4, 26, 27
airstairs 15
autopilot 19, 30

baggage 6, 7, 14, 17
baggage container 17
baggage hold 30
brake 20

cabin 6, 7, 16, 17, 22
cabin door 4, 6, 14, 15, 23
cargo doors 29
cockpit 19, 30
combustion chamber 10, 11
compressor 10, 11

computer 18, 19
control column 19, 30

elevator 12, 13, 19, 30
emergency exit 22
emergency slide 23
engine 5, 10, 11, 13, 23, 27, 28

fin 5, 7, 12, 13, 27, 30
fire extinguisher 23
flap 8, 9, 18, 30
flight deck 4, 6, 14, 15, 18, 19, 23, 30
fly-by-wire 18
fuel 8, 11, 18, 28
fuselage 5, 6, 7, 13, 14, 20, 21, 26, 27, 30

galley 24, 25, 30

hold 7, 14, 17, 25, 29

instrument panel 18, 19

jet engine 10, 11, 31

life jacket 22
life raft 23, 31

overhead locker 16, 23
oxygen mask 23

propeller engine 28, 31
pylon 10, 31

radar 18, 31
radar screen 18, 19
rib 7, 8, 12, 13, 31
rivet 6, 7, 31

rudder 5, 12, 13, 19, 31

seat 4, 7, 16, 17, 19, 27
slat 8, 9, 18, 31
spar 8, 12, 13, 31
spoiler 9, 31

tailplane 5, 7, 12, 13, 27, 31
trolley 24, 25
turbine 10, 11
turbofan 10, 11, 31

undercarriage 5, 7, 20, 21, 27, 28, 31

waste tank 25
wheel 20, 21, 28, 29
window 5, 14, 15
wing 5, 7, 8, 9, 10, 12, 20, 21, 26